structures
and buildings

© Aladdin Books Ltd 1994
Designed and produced by
Aladdin Books Ltd
28 Percy Street
London W1P 9FF

ISBN 0-8050-3418-8

First published in
the United States in 1994 by
Twenty-First Century Books,
A Division of Henry Holt & Company, Inc.
115 West 18th Street
New York, NY 10011

Library of Congress
Catalog-in-Publication Data
Hawkes, Nigel.
      Structures and buildings / Nigel Hawkes – 1st ed.
      p. cm. – (New technology)
      Includes index.
      ISBN 0–8050–3418–8
      1. Structural engineering – Juvenile literature. 2. Buildings
– Juvenile literature. [1. Structural engineering. 2. Buildings.]
I. Title.   II. Series.
TA634.H38   1994   93-49068
624. 1–dc20   CIP
                                                     AC

Design
David West
Children's Book Design
Designers
Steve Woosnam-Savage
Flick Killerby
Editor
Suzanne Melia
Picture Research
Brooks Krikler Research
Illustration
Alex Pang

Printed in Belgium

new TECHNOLOGY

structures
and buildings

NIGEL HAWKES

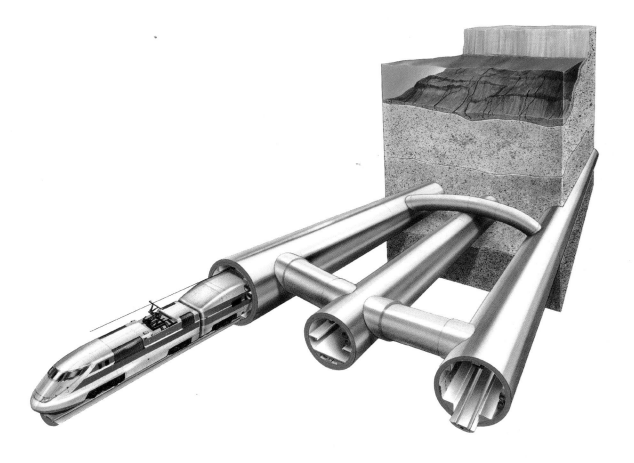

TWENTY-FIRST CENTURY BOOKS
A Division of Henry Holt and Company, Inc.

CONTENTS

Photocredits
*Abbreviations: t-top, m-middle, b-bottom,
l-left, r-right*
*Cover t, 22: Sandia; cover bl, 4, 4-5, 12-13 all:
Future Systems; cover br, 30b: Charles de Vere; 5b,
7, 8 both, 14 both, 15, 16-17 all, 18b, 19t, 20-21
all, 22-23t inset, 24b, 25 both, 26-27 all: Frank
Spooner Pictures; 11: Richard Rogers Partnership;
15t: Eamon O'Mahony/Richard Rogers Partnership;
18ml, 18-19, 19b, 22-23 background: Science Photo
Library; 22-23b inset: SERI; 24-25: NASA; 28-29
all, 30t: Spectrum Colour Library.*

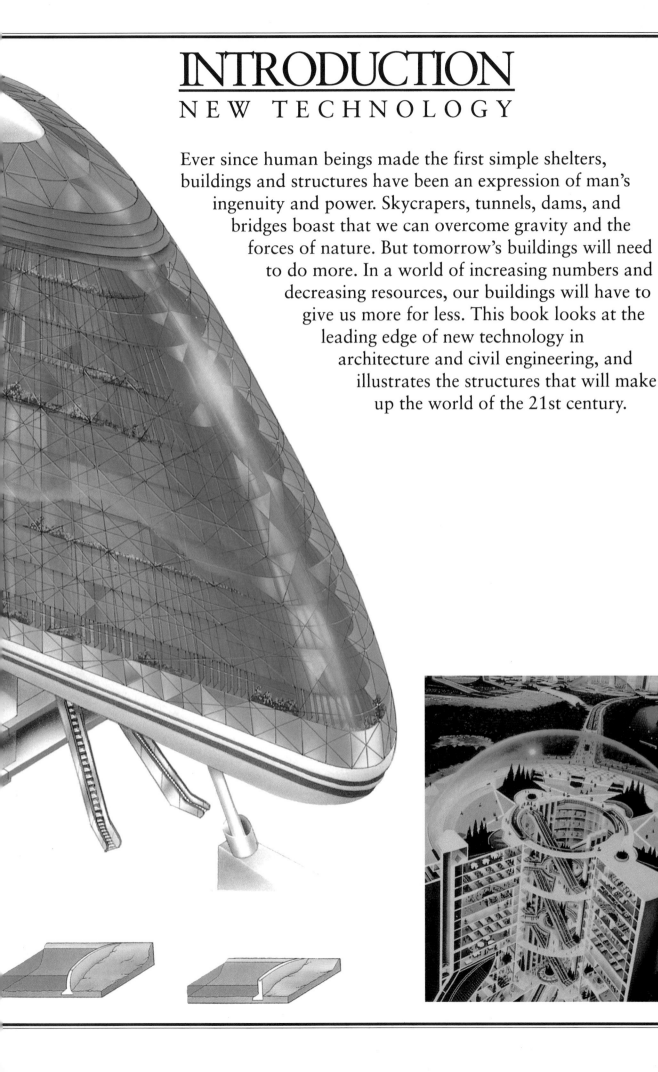

INTRODUCTION
NEW TECHNOLOGY

Ever since human beings made the first simple shelters, buildings and structures have been an expression of man's ingenuity and power. Skycrapers, tunnels, dams, and bridges boast that we can overcome gravity and the forces of nature. But tomorrow's buildings will need to do more. In a world of increasing numbers and decreasing resources, our buildings will have to give us more for less. This book looks at the leading edge of new technology in architecture and civil engineering, and illustrates the structures that will make up the world of the 21st century.

SKYSCRAPER

HIGHER AND HIGHER

The skyscraper, symbol of 20th century building, is about to soar still higher. Plans are afoot for buildings that will rise more than half a mile high, almost double the height of the world's tallest building today, the 1,454-foot *Sears Building* in Chicago. A team of Japanese architects has designed a gigantic pyramid that would provide offices and homes for a million people, and stand one and a quarter miles high. Behind the push toward ever-larger buildings is the scarcity of space, acute in Tokyo where land prices are the highest in the world. But huge buildings present new problems of safety, stability, and rapid movement between floors.

Japan's big five construction companies – Shimuzu, Taisei, Kajima, Takenaka, and Obayashi – all have plans for huge towers. Shimuzu's TRY 2004 is a pyramid one and a quarter-miles high, while Taisei has designed X-Seed 4000, a two-and-a-half-miles, high building shaped like Mount Fuji (below).

Helical bands

THE HIGHEST EVER

THE MILLENNIUM TOWER

The *Millennium Tower*, to be built in Tokyo and designed by British architect Sir Norman Foster, will be 2,500 feet high, on a base as big as Tokyo's *Olympic Stadium*. The building is round, which reduces wind pressure. This gives the building stability – like the trunk of a giant oak. It has five zones containing restaurants, theaters, and stores, separated by six "sky centers" which allow daylight into the building. Load is carried to the outside of the structure by transfer girders at each sky center, while the surface of the tower is covered by helical bands to carry the vertical load and prevent any swaying.

Wind

Transfer girders

Wind pressure reduced by round walls

Load

Skycenter

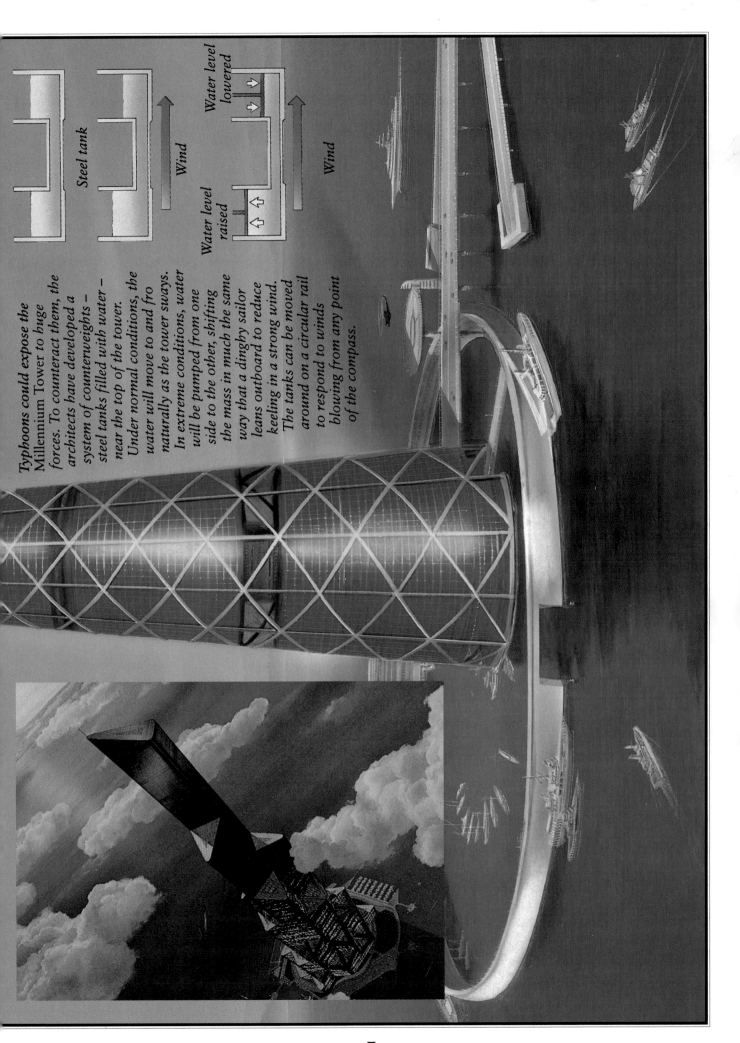

Typhoons could expose the Millennium Tower to huge forces. To counteract them, the architects have developed a system of counterweights – steel tanks filled with water – near the top of the tower. Under normal conditions, the water will move to and fro naturally as the tower sways. In extreme conditions, water will be pumped from one side to the other, shifting the mass in much the same way that a dinghy sailor leans outboard to reduce keeling in a strong wind. The tanks can be moved around on a circular rail to respond to winds blowing from any point of the compass.

Steel tank

Wind

Water level lowered

Water level raised

Wind

TUNNELS
UNDER THE CHANNEL

A dream for nearly 200 years, the tunnel under the English Channel between France and Britain is finally a reality. Construction began in 1986, and the tunnel was essentially complete by the end of 1993, at a cost of $12 billion. Of the total length of 30 miles, 23 miles lies under the sea, drilled through chalk some 50 to 150 feet below the seabed. It consists of three separate tunnels, two to take trains and the third to provide ventilation, access for service vehicles, and an escape route for passengers. The tunnel will carry three types of trains: high-speed intercity passenger trains, double-decker shuttle trains taking cars through in 35 minutes, and long-distance freight services.

The two shuttle terminals are in Kent, England and near Calais in France. The terminals are designed to enable cars and trucks to be loaded quickly. The passenger trains will link London to a growing network of high-speed lines in Europe.

Boring machine

Conveyor belt

Cylinder

Behind the boring machine is a cylinder, that grips the rock and steers the tunnel in the right direction by pushing against the wall of chalk. A conveyor belt carries the rock backward, onto trains that remove it from the tunnel.

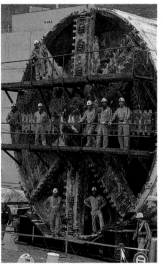

The tunnel was bored using huge machines weighing over 540 tons. On the front face of each were 100 cutting "rollers" and 200 picking teeth, made of tungsten (a type of metal). The face rotated at up to three times a minute, advancing about 5 inches in that time.

Shuttle trains will include 13 double-decker wagons, each able to take 120 cars, and 13 single-deck wagons for trucks and trailers. Passengers will remain in their vehicles during the crossing.

Shuttle train

The two main tunnels are linked to the service tunnel every 1,230 feet by cross-passages, and by smaller ducts every 820 feet, which allow air driven forward by the piston effect of the train to escape. The tunnel was bored from both sides of the Channel at the same time, using laser beams to guide the boring machines, ensuring that the tunnels met exactly.

The company *Eurotunnel* has been given a 65-year contract to run the tunnel, until it becomes the property of the British and French governments. Investors are sure that it is a profitable investment, but the ferries will provide stiff competition.

Beneath the floor of the Channel lies a bed of chalk, and below that a deep layer of chalk marl, which is a mixture of clay and chalk, dotted with regions of flint. Soft and easily cut, the chalk marl is perfect rock to tunnel through, enabling the company that dug the tunnel, TransManche Link, to use huge full-face boring machines. Nearer the French side, the tunnel runs through upper chalk, but a seal between the cutting head of the machine and the cylinder behind it stopped the water from seeping through.

Service tunnel

Forecasting how many people will use the tunnel is extremely difficult, because it depends on price, convenience, and how other forms of transportation compete.

Each of the main tunnels is 25 feet in diameter, about the size of a two-story house, while the service tunnel is 16 feet in diameter. The left-hand tunnel (as we look at it here) will carry the trains from Britain to France, with the trains in the right tunnel running the other way.

TOMIGAYA II
TOTAL ENERGY BUILDING

The typical office building of the 1970s and 1980s was a glass box, isolated from its surroundings and made habitable by expensive air conditioning.

Architects are now turning away from this in search of buildings that are in tune with the environment, using the sun and the wind to provide their energy. *Tomigaya II*, designed by the British architect, Sir Richard Rogers and colleagues, for a site overlooking Yoyogi Park in central Tokyo, is designed to be self-sufficient in energy, reducing running costs. It is a tower with the services, such as the elevators, split off into a separate stack, which acts as a chimney to extract stale air. The southern side of the building is fully glazed, but has adjustable shades.

The concrete structure of Tomigaya II is exposed to act as a heat absorber, and water around the deep basement serves the same purpose. In summer it is used to provide cooling, and in winter to warm the cool incoming air.

The air in Tokyo is heavily polluted, so fresh air is drawn in high up the service stack and filtered. The building is able to respond to the conditions outside.

Wind turbine

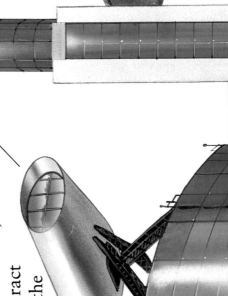

MOVING THE AIR
AUTOMATIC AIR CONDITIONING

The air conditioning system at *Tomigaya II* uses the chimney effect of the tall stack. The sun and the wind draw air up the stack, allowing stale, hot air from the building to rise and emerge from the top. The effect is to draw in fresh air from the outside, through an inlet halfway up the stack where it is cleaner than at ground level. This incoming air can then be cooled in summer, or heated in winter, by passing it through heat exchangers in the deep basement, which remain unaffected by outside temperatures. The incoming air is then circulated around.

Wind

Sunlight

Stale air

Heat exchangers

Air circulated around

Fresh air

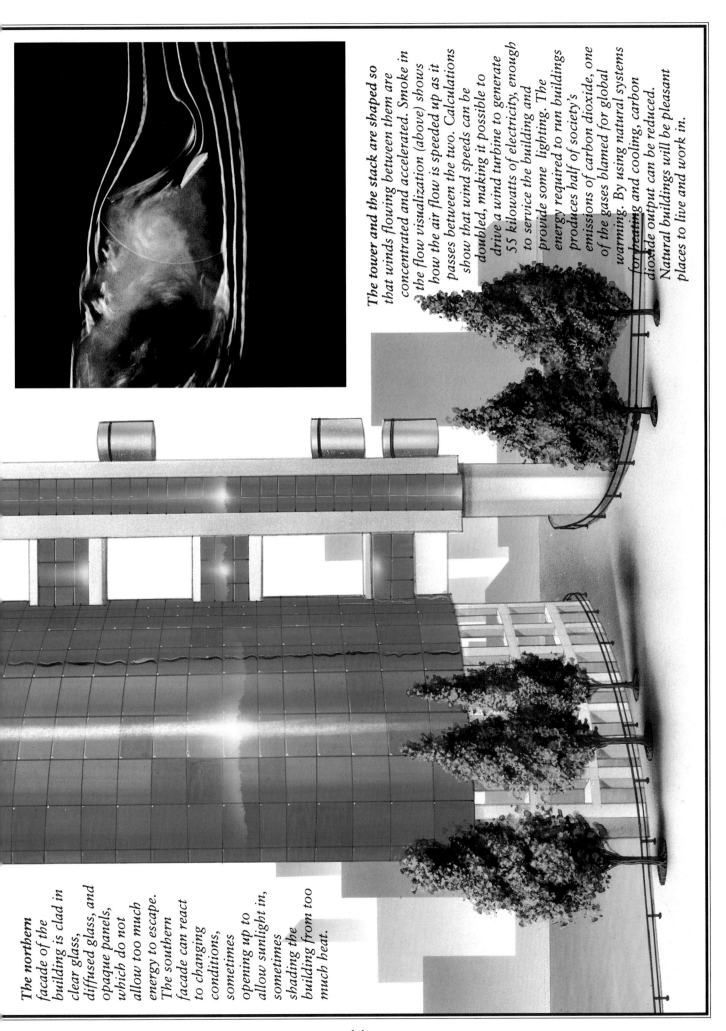

The northern facade of the building is clad in clear glass, diffused glass, and opaque panels, which do not allow too much energy to escape. The southern facade can react to changing conditions, sometimes opening up to allow sunlight in, sometimes shading the building from too much heat.

The tower and the stack are shaped so that winds flowing between them are concentrated and accelerated. Smoke in the flow visualization (above) shows how the air flow is speeded up as it passes between the two. Calculations show that wind speeds can be doubled, making it possible to drive a wind turbine to generate 55 kilowatts of electricity, enough to service the building and provide some lighting. The energy required to run buildings produces half of society's emissions of carbon dioxide, one of the gases blamed for global warming. By using natural systems for heating and cooling, carbon dioxide output can be reduced. Natural buildings will be pleasant places to live and work in.

GREEN BUILDING
THE CONTROLLED OFFICE

One of the most unusual offices ever designed is the *Green Building*, **a 12-story egg on a tripod.** Designed in 1990 by an architectural firm in London, it is a futuristic design that is unlikely ever to be built. However, its architects insist that it could be, and that it would work. The entire building is supported on three huge legs, constructed like the legs of an oil platform, which run right through the building to its tip. The weight of the floors and the facades is carried from the tip by a series of ties to the outer edges, like the support of the hoops in a hooped skirt.

The floors of the building are hollow steel boxes stiffened by plates, like the deck of a modern road bridge. Natural air flow is created by an open space, or atrium, up the center of the building, and aided by the flow of wind across the top of the atrium.

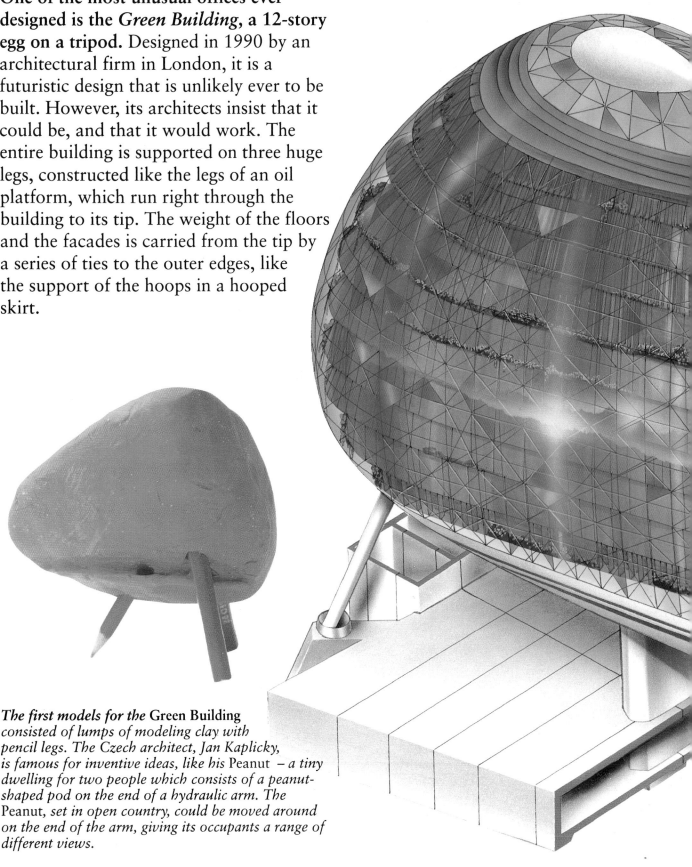

The first models for the Green Building *consisted of lumps of modeling clay with pencil legs. The Czech architect, Jan Kaplicky, is famous for inventive ideas, like his* Peanut – a tiny dwelling for two people which consists of a peanut-shaped pod on the end of a hydraulic arm. The Peanut, *set in open country, could be moved around on the end of the arm, giving its occupants a range of different views.*

Almost all parts of the building can get natural light, thanks to the large areas of glass. Each floor has tilting plastic mirrors that can be used to reflect sunlight right into the middle of the building, just below the ceiling. Light deflectors in the ceiling scatter this light downward, enabling all parts of the office to be naturally lit.

The whole of the Green Building *is clad in glass, which could make it unpleasantly hot on sunny days. To prevent this, fabric blinds can be lowered from inside the building. On cloudy days, the blinds can be raised.*

The object of the Green Building *is to achieve an office controlled by its occupants, not by automatic systems. Though it may never be built, its ideas have already been incorporated into other buildings.*

V E N T I L A T I O N
H O W   I T   W O R K S

One of the most original parts of the *Green Building* is its ventilation. Traditional houses get fresh air by opening windows, but in cities this cannot be done because the streets are too noisy. The *Green Building* uses the chimney effect to draw in air at the base of the egg.

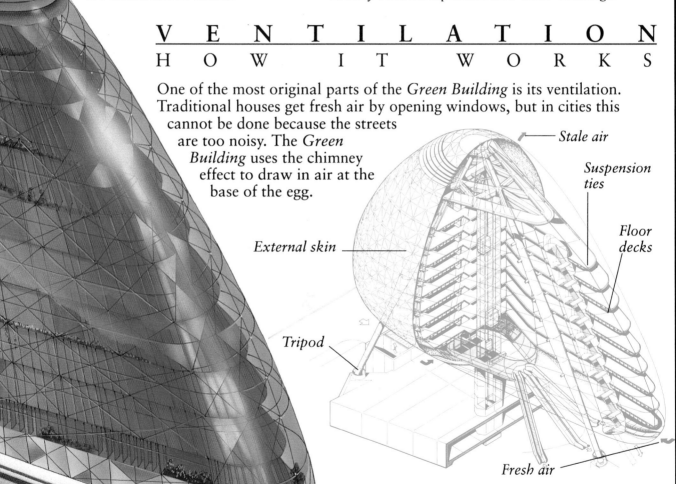

Stale air

Suspension ties

Floor decks

External skin

Tripod

Fresh air

The air is circulated in a narrow space between a sealed outer glass skin and an inner skin, also of glass, which can be opened like a window from the inside. The amount of fresh air is controlled entirely by the occupants, who can open and close the windows as they wish. Heat pumps can provide both heating and cooling if needed, and can redistribute heat from hotter to cooler areas. The sealed outer skin keeps the building quiet.

FUTURE CITIES
DESIGNING BETTER CITIES

Most of the world's population live in cities; and the cities we live in were almost all built before the invention of the car, the telephone, or electricity.

As a result, most cities are congested and polluted, and use energy inefficiently. Designing better cities is difficult because technology moves so fast: what makes sense on the drawing board may be out of date by the time the city is built. To escape from 19th century squalor, 20th century planners went for clean "garden cities" in which workplaces and homes were placed far apart. That forced people into cars, replacing factory pollution with exhaust fumes. Housing developments on the edges of cities provided good houses, but a boring environment that bred crime and disillusionment. *Lu Jia Zui*, a new plan for a district of Shanghai by the Richard Rogers Partnership, attempts to design a future city without these problems. Grouped around a park, *Lu Jia Zui* will

One solution to expanding urban populations could be to build out into the sea (below). Land has been reclaimed from the sea in the past, but the concept of a floating city – like a futuristic Venice – looks more and more probable. Reclaimed land could also provide the wide open spaces of parkland that may no longer exist in the older cities.

be served by steetcars and a light rail system, with frequent stops so that nobody will have to walk more than a quarter of a mile. The plan for *Lu Jia Zui* is flexible, to allow for change. A computer program allows changes in population, parking, energy-use, and the

movement of people to be analyzed and incorporated into the design. Housing and commercial developments are mixed in all six sections of the city. To maximize the daylight admitted to the buildings, a model was tested for summer and winter conditions.

Lu Jia Zui (right) will lie close to the famous Shanghai waterfront, the Bund. A light rail system will circulate around the central area, with parking for cars, and connections to the Shanghai subway.

S A V I N G   S P A C E
G O I N G   U N D E R G R O U N D

As the population of the world increases, space has become more and more valuable. Building downward instead of upward is one solution to an over-populated and over-polluted environment. This vision of the future (below) shows what an underground city might look like. Shielded from the outside weather conditions by a huge, glass dome, the underground city can create its own climatic conditions. Air from the outside could be cleaned and filtered before being pumped around the multi-story city, while natural light penetrates the building through a central atrium. Natural insulation from the surrounding earth would help to save the energy usually needed to heat or cool a conventional building above the surface.

Energy (right) would be provided both as heat, and as electricity, with all the buildings designed to be energy-efficient. The buildings have been arranged to maximize natural light, which cuts energy costs by 15 percent. All areas of the city are within easy reach of open spaces, with private cars banned from the inner areas.

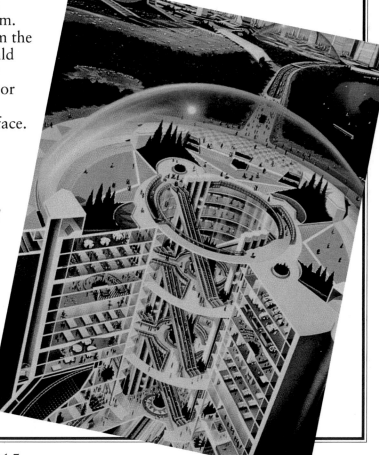

AIRPORTS
USING NEW LAND

In 1925, a grass strip at Kai Tak in Hong Kong became the territory's airport.
This single runway is much improved and extended, but is now surrounded by high-rise buildings, which make landing there an exciting experience. Kai Tak is the third busiest cargo airport in the world, and the fourth busiest for passengers. Little further expansion is possible, so a new airport is being built at Chek Lap Kok, a small island that will be totally flattened in one of the biggest civil engineering projects in the world today. At a cost of $16 billion, a two-runway airport will be built on Chek Lap Kok and more than 2,270 acres of land reclaimed from the sea. New roads, an airport railroad, a major docks development, and a new town for 200,000 people are also part of the ambitious plan.

Construction of the airport will begin when the site is fully prepared and leveled. The first runway should be ready by 1997, and by 2011 the airport is expected to handle 50 million passengers a year, more than double the capacity at Kai Tak.

The island of Chek Lap Kok and the island of Lam Chau will be flattened to 20 or 25 feet. This will provide only a quarter of the area needed however. The rest will be land reclaimed from the sea. This involves removing millions of cubic feet of soft marine mud and replacing it with marine sand, to form a solid base. Every day, the world's largest dredging fleet shifts 14 million cubic feet of material from around the island, enough to cover a football field to a height of 200 feet. Another huge land reclamation project will create the space for the new town of Tung Chung, where airport workers will live.

The Port and Airport Development Strategy of Hong Kong (PADS) is designed to maintain the city's position at the hub of Southeast Asia, one of the world's fastest-developing regions. In 1997, when the first runway will open at Chek Lap Kok, the territory will return to the Chinese after a century of British administration. Beijing will inherit the world's most dynamic city, a center of finance, industry, and commerce whose influence is out of all proportion to its size. Hong Kong's container port, already the world's busiest, will be expanded.

Hong Kong has a total land area of only 400 square miles, and 70 percent of that is mountainous. To provide the space for its huge developments, land needs to be created from the sea by shifting in huge quantities of marine sand in dredgers. The underlying mud must be strengthened by laying vertical drains to remove water. In some places, the whole depth of mud is removed and replaced by sand, which is made firmer by inserting vibrating metal probes. These agitate the sand particles and make them pack more closely together to form a solid base. To protect the newly-created land, seawalls are usually needed. More than a mile of seawall is already in place.

As engineers learn how to reclaim land from the sea, floating airports could become a reality in the future. A floating airport takes advantage of the space available out at sea, preventing noise pollution in built-up areas and offering spacious facilities.

BIOSPHERE 2
THE GREENHOUSE EARTH

In the desert, 40 miles north of Tucson, Arizona, a model of the earth has been created inside a huge greenhouse. *Biosphere 2* was home for two years to eight volunteers who survived – more or less – on what they could grow within the 3,000 acres of the building. Their aim was to prove that life was sustainable inside the sealed mini-world, and to carry out research for the possible construction of future space colonies.

The basic structure of Biosphere 2 consists of ribs of steel linked together, with glass sheets stuck directly to the ribs with silicone sealant. As well as being an experiment, Biosphere 2 was a tourist attraction; 200,000 visitors a year payed to come and gaze through the glass.

Abigail Alling prepares to dive into the Ocean biome (above). Not everything inside was hard work, however. The occupants had a recreation room (below) where they could relax, talk, and play games.

Inside *Biosphere 2* were small-scale copies of the oceans, grasslands, forests, marshes, and deserts found in Biosphere 1 – the earth itself. The eight "Biospherians" shared the space with 3,800 other plant and animal species, designed to create as balanced an ecosystem as possible. They had problems, from crop failures to mites, and all of them lost a great deal of weight.

Biosphere 2 *consists of two linked glasshouses, the circular domed agricultural space and the pyramidal section housing the artificial habitats. To allow for air inside to expand and contract with the changing temperature,* Biosphere 2 *was connected to a "lung," a huge rubber bag in a dome that could fill and empty.*

The most serious problem was a steadily declining level of oxygen inside *Biosphere 2*, which exposed its occupants to conditions similar to those experienced 15,000 feet up a mountain. The plants ought to have created enough oxygen, but for reasons so far unexplained, were unable to do so. Eventually, more oxygen was pumped in, breaking the original promises, but preventing the Biospherians' health from suffering permanent damage. Remarkably, there was only one serious argument in the whole period.

The savannah biome is the area inside Biosphere 2 *where the world's grasslands are modeled. 45 species of grass were planted. Colonies of ants and termites provided a natural balance. The other biomes were a rainforest, an ocean with a coral reef, and a desert. Many species died, but some survived.*

UNDERWATER
BUILDING UNDER THE SEA

The world's first underwater hotel, the *Jules Verne Underwater Lodge*, opened in Key Largo, Florida, in 1986. For the first time it was possible for people to stay 30 feet under the sea. The lodge is over 50 feet long and 20 feet wide, and has space for six people. The rooms have large windows with panoramic views of the underwater world outside. The lodge is connected to a control center on land by a cable which delivers air, power, and communications for television and phones.

Many hoteliers believe that the unexplored world of the sea offers a new opportunity. They envisage plastic tunnels built across the seabed, enabling visitors to walk along on the bottom of the ocean observing the wildlife. Using scuba diving equipment, the more adventurous may make safaris into the open sea.

Access to the lodge is through an open space between the living and sleeping areas. Guests take a quick course in skin diving, then plunge into the pool and emerge in the lodge. It's safe, but exciting.

The lodge, seen out of the water, was originally a research habitat capable of supporting people for weeks at a depth of 100 feet.

The interior has been designed to provide luxury accommodation. Guests can cook their own food in the galley kitchen, or call a "mermaid" to help. At night, they can tune into TV or play back their own sub-sea videos. The lodge's environment is human-controlled.

Modern aquariums, like Sea World in San Diego, California (left), provide an idea of what undersea walkways will be like. Here visitors can watch sharks in complete safety through the unbreakable windows. But such structures could only be built in calm and shallow waters, such as tropical lagoons. Underwater restaurants are also planned, to which people would be ferried by submarine.

L U Z
SOLAR POWER STATION

The world's biggest solar power complex, *Luz,* **lies in the Mohave Desert, 140 miles northeast of Los Angeles.**

Six power plants, built over a period of ten years, generate huge amounts of power from the sun; sufficient energy for a city of 200,000 people. The sun's heat is collected by long, curved mirrors, guided by computers, and directed onto tubes of a synthetic oil. The oil is heated to 750°F, and used to heat water to produce the steam that drives the turbines.

At Sandia *test facility in New Mexico, a solar power plant uses mirrors to concentrate the sun's rays on a collector at the top of a tower.*

Solar One *power plant in California uses 1,800 mirrors to track the sun's movement and focus its light on the collector at the center of the plant.*

Although the *Luz* complex can generate huge amounts of electricity, it costs about 25 percent more than energy from a gas, or oil-fired plant. Although the energy itself is free, the plants are expensive to build and maintain. Solar plants based on photovoltaic cells, which convert sunlight directly into electricity, may be more economical in the long run, if cheaper and more efficient solar cells can be developed.

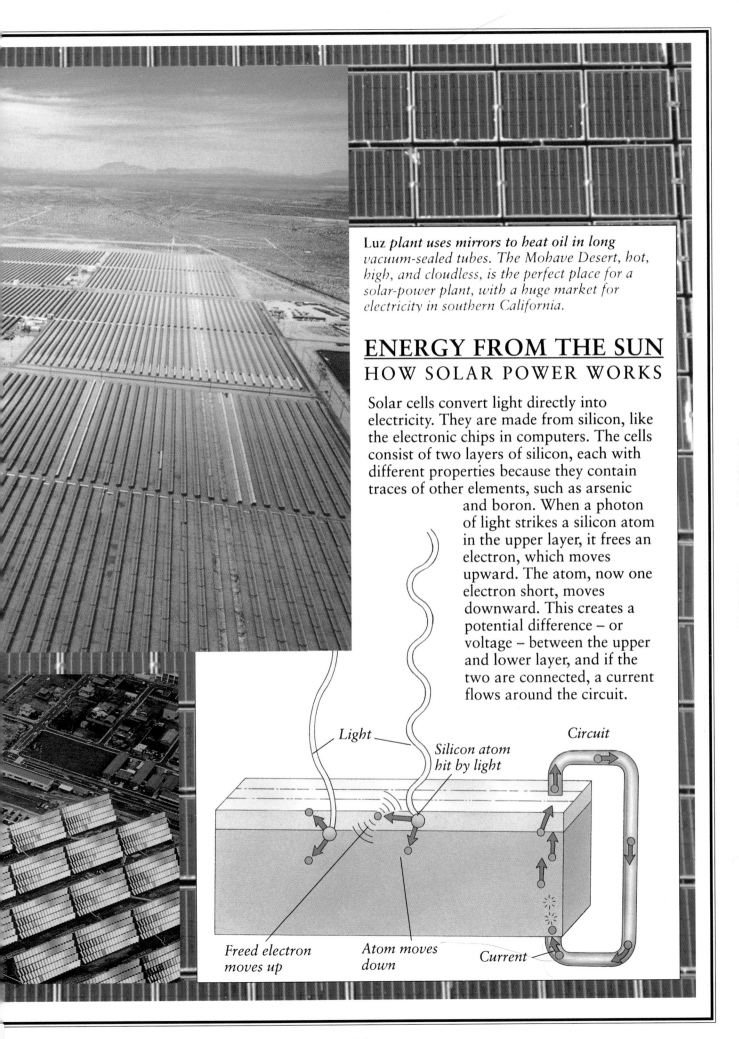

Luz plant uses mirrors to heat oil in long vacuum-sealed tubes. The Mohave Desert, hot, high, and cloudless, is the perfect place for a solar-power plant, with a huge market for electricity in southern California.

ENERGY FROM THE SUN
HOW SOLAR POWER WORKS

Solar cells convert light directly into electricity. They are made from silicon, like the electronic chips in computers. The cells consist of two layers of silicon, each with different properties because they contain traces of other elements, such as arsenic and boron. When a photon of light strikes a silicon atom in the upper layer, it frees an electron, which moves upward. The atom, now one electron short, moves downward. This creates a potential difference – or voltage – between the upper and lower layer, and if the two are connected, a current flows around the circuit.

Light

Silicon atom
hit by light

Circuit

Freed electron
moves up

Atom moves
down

Current

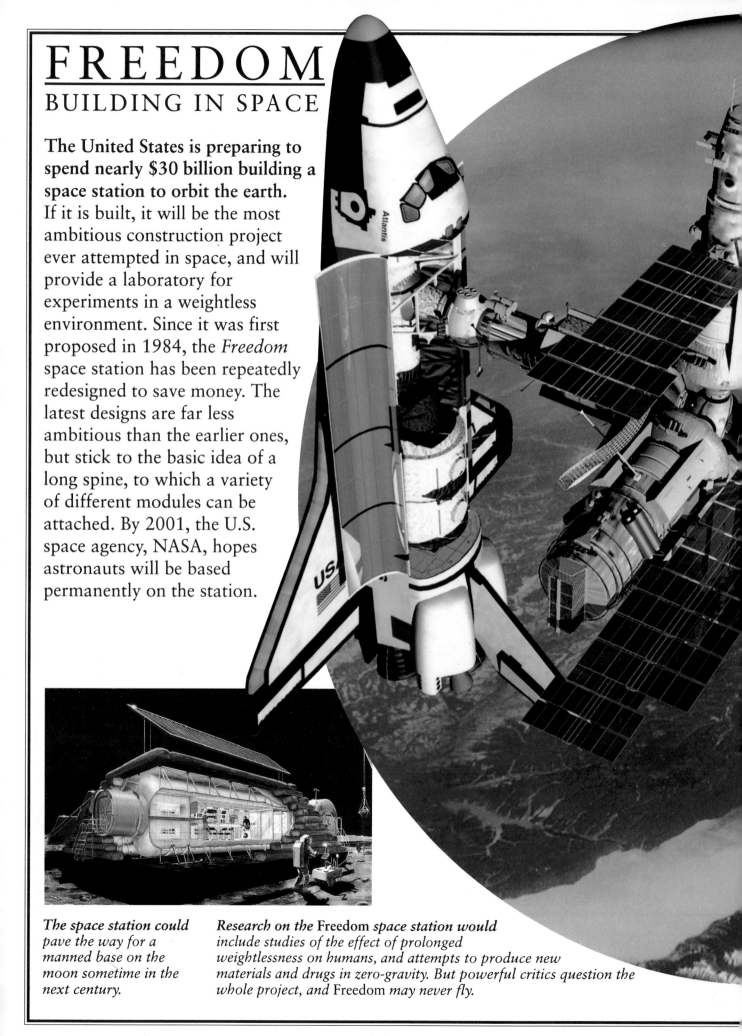

FREEDOM
BUILDING IN SPACE

The United States is preparing to spend nearly $30 billion building a space station to orbit the earth. If it is built, it will be the most ambitious construction project ever attempted in space, and will provide a laboratory for experiments in a weightless environment. Since it was first proposed in 1984, the *Freedom* space station has been repeatedly redesigned to save money. The latest designs are far less ambitious than the earlier ones, but stick to the basic idea of a long spine, to which a variety of different modules can be attached. By 2001, the U.S. space agency, NASA, hopes astronauts will be based permanently on the station.

The space station could pave the way for a manned base on the moon sometime in the next century.

Research on the Freedom *space station would include studies of the effect of prolonged weightlessness on humans, and attempts to produce new materials and drugs in zero-gravity. But powerful critics question the whole project, and* Freedom *may never fly.*

The first stage in building the station would be to create the basic structure and attach the solar panels. The space shuttle would be used to carry the U.S.-built modules to the station and attach them, with the international modules following.

The ultimate prize could be a base on Mars, the only planet in the solar system, apart from earth, which appears remotely habitable. The first manned visit to Mars is planned sometime in the next century.

Latest designs for Freedom, are a greatly simplified version of the original. One major change is the removal of costly windows.

ITAIPU DAM
A MODERN POWER STATION

Dams are the world's biggest structures, transforming nature in order to generate electricity and provide irrigation.

Itaipu, on the Parana River, which divides Brazil from Paraguay, stands more than 900 feet tall, the height of a 60-story building. Its 18 turbines were designed to produce more than a quarter of Brazil's power needs. Up to 28,000 workers were employed on the project, which together with another huge dam, the *Tucurui* on the Tocantins River in Amazonia, cost $23 billion. But even these massive projects will be dwarfed by the *Three Gorges* scheme on the Yangtze River in China. If this goes ahead it will flood 400 miles of river valley, displace more than a million people from their homes, and generate 18,000 megawatts of electricity. Such huge projects generate controversy because of their effects on the environment and on local people. Opposition to the Yangtse dam was one of the rallying cries at the democracy demonstrations in Beijing's Tiananmen Square in 1989, and Amazonian Indians have protested against plans for dams in Brazil. But dams are a cheap and effective source of electricity, and now provide about a fifth of the world's demand.

Dams are getting bigger and bigger. Of the world's ten highest dams, all but two have been built since 1970. Some dams, like Itaipu, *are built of concrete, and resist the pressure of the water simply by their own huge weight, or by bearing against the walls of the valley. But most dams are made of earth, rock, and clay, usually readily available on-site, piled into engineered embankments. They are cheaper, and can adjust to shifting ground or weak foundations much more easily.*

TYPES OF DAMS
DIFFERENT SHAPES

In a hydro-electric plant, the power of falling water is used to drive a turbine connected to a generator. Wherever possible, a dam is built at the mouth of a gorge or valley to force the waters of a river to pile up behind it to form a lake. In a typical embankment dam, a tunnel carries the water from behind the dam to turbines in the powerhouse. The greater the drop between the water level behind the dam and the turbines, the greater the force of water and the quantity of electricity generated.

Buttressed sraight dam

Embankment dam

Double curvature dam

Arch dam

CHRONOLOGY

2650 BC *The first of the Egyptian pyramids was built for King Djoser, who lived between 2668 and 2649 BC. For the next thousand years, every King of note was buried beneath a pyramid. The largest,* the Great Pyramid of Cheops, *completed in 2580 BC, was the world's tallest building for almost 4,000 years, until overtaken in 1307 by* Lincoln Cathedral *in England. It contains more than two million blocks of limestone, each weighing 2.25 tons.*

80 AD *The Colosseum was completed. Built to hold 50,000 spectators, it had 80 entrances. The Romans used the arch to create bridges and aqueducts, many of which survive to this day. They also built drains and roads, and created the tradition of civil engineering.*

300 BC *In the East, the Chinese built what is still the single greatest object ever created by man:* The Great Wall of China, *which snakes across China for 2,150 miles and took millions of men hundreds of years to build. Designed as a defense against the Mongols who came from the North, the wall runs along the tops of the mountains, dominating the high ground. The wall is 20-30 feet high, and 25 feet wide at the base. It also has watchtowers, which were built every few hundred yards.*

1100-1400 AD *After the fall of the Roman Empire, building design declined. But it emerged again in the Middle Ages with the building of the great Gothic cathedrals. In England,* Canterbury *and* Durham *cathedrals were begun in the early years of the 12th century. Domestic buildings of the period were made mostly of timber, with the gaps filled in with mud-and-wattle or bricks.*

1681 *The completion of* the Canal du Midi, *linking the Mediterranean to the Atlantic, was the first important canal of the modern age.*

1779 *The first bridge made of iron was built between 1777 and 1779*

The floor of the Colosseum *was made of wood with trap doors that led to animal cages.*

The Great Pyramids *at Giza*

across the Severn River at Ironbridge, England. It had a span of over 100 feet, and was made of cast iron ribs and arches, weighing a total of 341 tons.

1843 Tunnels were built for the canals, but the coming of the railroads made tunneling more important. The first tunnel under water was completed in 1843 by Mark Isambard Brunel, under the Thames River in London, England, after two huge floods had delayed the work. It was the first in a series

built by John and Washington Roebling, and completed in 1883, with a span of 1,596 feet.

1884 The use of steel in building made possible the skyscraper. The first steel-framed building was the ten-story Home Insurance *building in Chicago, built by William Jenney in 1884. The steel is supported without needing extremely thick walls at ground level.*

1930-31 The Empire State Building *in New York was built at*

The Empire State Building

The Greenwich foot tunnel was built in 1902

of railroad and foot tunnels to be built under the Thames. The Greenwich foot-tunnel *was opened in 1902 to allow dockers who worked at India Docks to walk through.*

1883 *One of the greatest of all suspension bridges was the* Brooklyn Bridge,

astonishing speed, using steel beams made in Pittsburgh, and delivered to the site on a relentless schedule. The 53,800 tons of beams were held together with rivets, heated and hammered home by crews working hundreds of feet up in the air. All 102 stories of

tall as the Eiffel Tower. What is more, they had to be floated from where they were built to their position in the ocean, and placed precisely, and gently on the bottom.

1992 Canary Wharf, Britain's tallest skyscraper, rises 800 feet above the docklands development in East London. Isolated as it is, Canary Wharf can be seen from more than 10 miles away, a light on top of its conical roof flashes to warn aircraft away. Big for London, Canary Wharf is a relative minnow in world terms. The world's tallest occupied building is the Sears Tower in Chicago,

The Golden Gate Bridge in San Francisco

the Empire State Building were erected within six months.

1937 The world's most famous bridge is the Golden Gate in San Francisco, which stretches 4,200 feet across the entrance to San Francisco Bay. The bridge was very difficult to build, because it is across what is virtually open sea, with strong tides.

1969-80 During the 1970s, The St. Gotthard road tunnel was built. A total of 730 men were employed, and 19 lost their lives during construction.

1971-88 The world's longest rail tunnel runs between the islands of Honshu and Hokkaido in Japan. Thirty four miles long and a minimum depth of 275

feet below the sea, the Seikan Tunnel was far harder to build than the Channel tunnel. The rock was volcanic, full of fissures and cracks that allowed water through, and digging took twice as long and cost ten times more than the initial estimate.

1981 The longest single span in the world is the Humber Bridge, built between 1972 and 1981 to provide a link across the Humber Estuary in England. Its span is 4,625 feet, and the bridge is suspended from towers made of reinforced concrete.

1978-81 Some of the biggest structures ever created are virtually invisible to most people. They are the

Canary Wharf is the tallest building in London.

production platforms used to extract oil from the North Sea. Made of steel or concrete, these oil platforms stand twice as tall as the Great Pyramid of Cheops and nearly as

at 1,420 feet, but the CN Tower, a TV tower in Toronto, is the tallest unsupported structure, at 1,822 feet. It has the world's highest restaurant, The Skypod.

GLOSSARY

Air Conditioning
System for heating or cooling air inside a building to ensure comfortable conditions.

Aqueduct
An above-ground artificial channel for carrying water.

Atrium
A large open space in the center of a building, often rising almost the full height. The top may be glazed to admit light.

Biosphere
The original Biosphere is the earth – literally the "life sphere."

Chalk
A soft rock formed originally from the shells of tiny sea creatures. Chemically it is calcium carbonate.

Container
A large box used for transporting many kinds of goods by sea. Containers are easily handled by cranes and more convenient than carrying goods loose.

Counterweight
A weight that is used to correct an imbalance, for example in a tall building.

Diffuser
A screen, such as a piece of cloth or frosted glass, that softens light or distributes light evenly.

Flow Visualization
The use of models to predict the flow of air through and around a building.

Girder
A horizontal, main structural member that supports the vertical loads of a building.

Heat Exchanger
A device for transferring heat from one substance to another. A radiator, which transfers heat from water to air, is an example.

Heat Pump
Machine for extracting heat from a source at one temperature and supplying it at another. Refrigerators are heat pumps that remove heat from their insides and release it outside.

Helical
Coil or spiral shaped. This is a very strong shape .

Jules Verne
19th century French writer, author of the book *20,000 Leagues Under the Sea*.

Load
The forces a structure is subjected to, due to weight or to wind pressure on the vertical surfaces.

Megawatt (MW)
A million watts (see Watt).

Watt
Unit of electrical power named after the engineer, James Watt. A light bulb might use 60 or 100 watts of electricity. A kilowatt equals 1000 watts, a megawatt, one million.

INDEX